Mike Tomlin

MIKE TOMLIN:

The Maestro of the Gridiron

Marlin M. Lawler

Mike Tomlin

All rights reserved. No part of this publication may be reproduced, distributed, or transmitted in any form or by any means, including photocopying, recording, or other electronic or mechanical methods, without the prior written permission of the publisher, except in the case of brief quotations embodied in critical reviews and certain other noncommercial uses permitted by copyright law.

Copyright © Marlin M. Lawler , 2024.

Mike Tomlin

TABLE OF CONTENTS

INTRODUCTION

CHAPTER 1: ORIGINS OF GREATNESS

1.1 Early Life in Hampton, Virginia

1.2 Formative Years at Denbigh High School

1.3 Academic and Athletic Journey at William & Mary

CHAPTER 2: EDUCATIONAL QUEST

2.1 Transition to Coaching at Virginia Military Institute

2.2 Coaching Roles at Various Universities

2.3 Evolving Leadership Traits and Tactical Acumen

CHAPTER 3: NFL BEGINNING

3.1 Early Career in the NFL Coaching Ranks

3.2 Lessons Learned and Skills Honed

3.3 Pathway to Becoming a Defensive Strategist

Mike Tomlin

CHAPTER 4: THE PITTSBURGH STEELERS ERA BEGINS

4.1 Appointment as Head Coach of the Pittsburgh Steelers

4.2 Impact on Team Dynamics and Culture

4.3 Setting the Stage for Success

CHAPTER 5: COACHING PHILOSOPHY UNVEILED

5.1 Emphasis on Unity and Discipline

5.2 Building a Winning Culture

5.3 Transformative Approach to Leadership

CHAPTER 6: ACHIEVEMENTS

6.1 Division Titles and Playoff Appearances

6.2 Super Bowl Victory in Super Bowl XLIII

6.3 Tomlin's Mark on Steelers' History

CHAPTER 7: LEADERSHIP BEYOND THE GAME

Mike Tomlin

7.1 Mentorship and Player Development

7.2 Advocacy for Social Causes

7.3 Inspirational Impact Beyond Football

CHAPTER 8: ENDURING LEGACY

8.1 Tomlin's Influence

8.2 Reflections on Coaching Philosophy

8.3 Contributions to Football's Pantheon of Greats

CONCLUSION

Mike Tomlin

INTRODUCTION

In the world of American football, where legendary stadiums ring with the sound of titanic collisions and fan fervor permeates every aspect of the game, one name is inextricably linked to perseverance, leadership, and a never-ending quest for greatness: Mike Tomlin. The narrative of this book tells the story of a man whose rise from the fields of Hampton, Virginia, to the head of the Pittsburgh Steelers epitomizes tenacity, perseverance, and the unwavering pursuit of excellence.

Michael Pettaway Tomlin, born on a serene March day in 1972, emerged from the heart of Hampton—a place where dreams weren't merely whispered but nurtured, where aspirations took flight amidst the echoes of the gridiron. From the corridors of Denbigh High School to the illustrious halls of William & Mary, his story

Mike Tomlin

burgeoned—a tale intertwined with a passion for the game that burned brighter than the Friday night lights.

His collegiate tenure was not just an academic pursuit, but a crucible wherein leadership traits, strategic acumen, and an understanding of the game's intricacies were meticulously forged. It was within these formative years that the seeds of a future coaching maestro were sown—a destiny bound to the sidelines, etching plays and shaping futures.

Mike Tomlin's rise to the top of American football wasn't a coincidental ascent; rather, it was a route he forged via tenacity, devotion, and an unwavering love for the game. Every step he took, from his modest beginnings as a graduate assistant at Virginia Military Institute to the hallowed halls of the NFL, left his mark as a leader—humble but unwavering, tactical but compassionate.

The Pittsburgh Steelers beckoned—a storied franchise, rich in history and brimming with legacy. In 2007,

Mike Tomlin

Tomlin assumed the mantle of head coach, marking the genesis of an era characterized not merely by victories on the field but by the fostering of a culture—a culture steeped in unity, discipline, and an insatiable hunger for success.

Under his stewardship, the Steelers weren't just a team; they were a testament to resilience, a symbol of camaraderie, and a living embodiment of Tomlin's coaching philosophy. Multiple division titles, playoff appearances, and the crowning glory of a Super Bowl victory in Super Bowl XLIII were not just conquests in the record books but monuments in the annals of his coaching legacy.

Yet, Mike Tomlin's impact transcends the metrics of wins and losses. It's a narrative woven with threads of mentorship, advocacy, and a commitment to making a difference beyond the confines of the football field. His influence extends far beyond X's and O's, shaping not just players but inspiring countless individuals to strive for greatness, both in sports and in life.

Mike Tomlin

Mike Tomlin's life is explored in great detail in this chronicle, which explores his many facets and reveals a tapestry of leadership, tenacity, and unwavering devotion to his beloved sport. As we take you on a journey through the highs and lows, victories and setbacks, and the lasting legacy of a man whose name is synonymous with American football, we hope to demonstrate the enduring strength of the human spirit.

This introduction sets the stage for the immersive exploration of Mike Tomlin's journey, emphasizing his beginnings, his coaching philosophy, and the impact he's had on the sport and those around him.

Mike Tomlin

CHAPTER 1: ORIGINS OF GREATNESS

The birthplace of Mike Tomlin was in the center of Hampton, Virginia, where a young dreamer's soul was prepared for greatness. His romantic relationship with football began in the bustling streets of his hometown, where the sound of resolve triumphed over doubts. He was born on a clear March day in 1972.

Mike Tomlin's journey was an inspiration to tenacity and determination from the beginning. His early years at Denbigh High School served as a blank canvas for him to express his love of the game. Here, under Hampton's blue skies, the gridiron evolved from a field to a place where hopes were raised, where dreams were realized, and where a future coach started honing his craft under the watchful eyes of mentors and teammates.

Mike Tomlin

The hallways of William and Mary saw Tomlin's development—a testing ground where intellectual endeavors entwined with an emerging love for football. It wasn't just about getting a degree during his time at this prestigious university; it was also a time when leadership qualities began to emerge, when strategic thinking began to take hold, and when his passion for the game intensified into a burning desire.

In addition to knowledge, Hampton's son came out of the academic furnace with a vision of leadership, an appreciation of the subtleties of the game, and an unwavering resolve to make a lasting impression on the football world.

Mike Tomlin's origins of greatness were forged within the embrace of Hampton's community spirit—a place where dreams weren't just encouraged but fostered, where aspirations weren't just envisioned but realized. It was amidst the soul-stirring rhythms of this vibrant locale that a young boy's aspirations transcended the

Mike Tomlin

boundaries of possibility, laying the groundwork for a future etched in the annals of American football history.

From the streets of Hampton to the helm of one of the NFL's most storied franchises, Mike Tomlin's journey embodies the ethos of a dreamer-turned-leader—a testament to the enduring power of passion, resilience, and the unwavering pursuit of greatness.

His roots went beyond a simple geographic location; they were ingrained in the principles, the character, and the tenacity of a community that fed the fires of ambition. This fire would flare brilliantly on the great NFL stages, lighting the way for countless aspirants who would come after him.

1.1 Early Life in Hampton, Virginia

Mike Tomlin's birth and early life in Hampton, Virginia, set the stage for the emergence of a future gridiron

Mike Tomlin

luminary, shaping not just the trajectory of a young boy's life but also infusing his spirit with the values and resilience characteristic of the region.

Born on a serene March day in 1972, in the heart of Hampton, Virginia, Mike Tomlin's story began amidst the backdrop of a community steeped in tradition, pride, and a deep-rooted love for the game of football. The air was filled not just with the crispness of spring but also with the echoes of determination that would come to define the young Tomlin's journey.

Hampton, a city known for its rich history and cultural vibrancy, provided the perfect canvas for the budding aspirations of a future football star. Its streets, woven with tales of ambition and perseverance, were the playgrounds where Tomlin's love for the game flourished. From spirited games played in local parks to the resounding cheers of supportive friends and family, the gridiron became more than just a field—it was a realm where dreams began to take shape.

Mike Tomlin

Within the embrace of Hampton's close-knit community, Tomlin's formative years were nurtured by the values of hard work, determination, and a steadfast commitment to excellence. These values weren't merely inherited; they were woven into the very fabric of daily life—a tapestry that instilled in him the ethos of resilience and a relentless pursuit of one's passions.

As the son of a single mother, Tomlin's early life was colored with lessons in perseverance and resilience—values that would become foundational in his journey toward achieving greatness. The challenges of a single-parent upbringing were met with unwavering resolve, instilling in him an indomitable spirit that would later define his coaching style and leadership philosophy.

Mike Tomlin was raised in the heart of Hampton, where the community was warm and dreams were big. His early years there paved the way for a future filled with leadership, football skills, and a commitment to making a lasting impression on both the game and the lives of those he touched.

Mike Tomlin

Hampton, with its vibrant tapestry of culture, history, and community spirit, served as the nurturing ground where the roots of greatness were planted—a place that shaped the character, resilience, and unwavering determination of a young boy who would one day stand as a towering figure in the world of American football.

1.2 Formative Years at Denbigh High School

Mike Tomlin's early years at Hampton, Virginia's Denbigh High School were a pivotal period that set the stage for the development of a future gridiron legend. In the corridors of this prestigious university, among teammates and under the tutelage of mentors, Tomlin's love of football blossomed, laying the groundwork for an adventure that would reverberate throughout the annals of American sports history.

A young Tomlin found himself engrossed in the world of football at Denbigh High School, which was more than

Mike Tomlin

just a place of instruction. It was a furnace where hopes were nourished and dreams took off. He developed his skills on the sacred grounds of the school's athletic fields, where the sounds of commitment and tenacity resonated through every practice, every match, every triumphant and difficult moment.

Amidst the vibrant energy of Denbigh High School's athletic programs, Tomlin's passion for the gridiron was ignited, his skills on full display as he showcased not just his athletic prowess but also the leadership traits that would define his future. As a young player, he exhibited an unmatched determination, a hunger to improve, and an unwavering commitment to his craft—a testament to the values instilled in him during his early years in Hampton.

The football fields of Denbigh High School served as a stage where Tomlin's talent blossomed, catching the eye of mentors and coaches who recognized his potential. More than just a player, he exemplified the qualities of a leader—a beacon of inspiration for his teammates, a

Mike Tomlin

strategist on the field, and a resilient competitor who approached every game with unyielding determination.

Beyond the touchdowns and tackles, Denbigh High School provided an environment that fostered camaraderie, teamwork, and the indomitable spirit needed to navigate the challenges both on and off the field. The lessons learned during those formative years weren't just about winning games; they were about perseverance, discipline, and the values that would later shape Tomlin's coaching philosophy.

When Tomlin was a young athlete at Denbigh High School, his experiences in the highs and lows of competitive sports shaped the resiliency, work ethic, and unwavering dedication that would serve as the cornerstone of his success in the future. Within these halls, the groundwork was established for an illustrious American football career where Mike Tomlin's remarkable journey would be marked by victories, significant anniversaries, and moments that would forever define his legacy.

Mike Tomlin

1.3 Academic and Athletic Journey at William & Mary

Mike Tomlin's academic and athletic journey at the College of William & Mary stands as a testament to the fusion of scholarly pursuits and gridiron excellence. Within the venerable walls of this esteemed institution, Tomlin's path unfolded—a journey that not only honed his skills on the football field but also cultivated the intellect, leadership, and resilience that would become hallmarks of his illustrious career.

The College of William & Mary, steeped in academic excellence and sporting tradition, provided the perfect backdrop for Tomlin's growth—nurturing not just his passion for football but also fostering an environment that valued scholastic achievements alongside athletic prowess. As he traversed the corridors of learning, Tomlin's commitment to both his studies and his athletic endeavors was unwavering, setting the stage for a balanced approach that would define his future endeavors.

Amidst the pursuit of academic excellence, Tomlin's dedication to the game of football remained steadfast. His tenure as a student-athlete was a testament to the art of balancing the rigors of academics with the demands of competitive sports. He excelled not only in the classroom but also on the field, showcasing not just his physical prowess but also his strategic acumen, leadership, and unwavering work ethic.

As a scholar and athlete at William & Mary, Tomlin's tenure wasn't solely defined by touchdowns and tackles. It was a period where the values of discipline, perseverance, and teamwork were ingrained, where the challenges faced on the field mirrored the trials encountered within the realm of academia. The lessons learned from both spheres intertwined, shaping a young Tomlin into a multifaceted individual—a student of the game and a student of life.

Mike Tomlin

William and Mary turned into the furnace that shaped Tomlin's personality; it was here that his strategic thinking developed, his leadership qualities were fostered, and the principles instilled in him during his early years found a home. A young man ready to make a lasting impression on the world of American football was shaped by the diverse experiences he had, including wins, losses, academic successes, and athletic accomplishments.

The College of William & Mary served as the incubator for Tomlin's growth—a space where academic pursuits converged with gridiron passion, fostering an environment that propelled him towards a future steeped in footballing excellence and leadership. As he journeyed through the corridors of this esteemed institution, the seeds of greatness were sown—seeds that would eventually blossom into an enduring legacy that transcended the realms of sports, academics, and leadership, embodying the epitome of the student-athlete ideal.

Mike Tomlin

CHAPTER 2: EDUCATIONAL QUEST

Mike Tomlin's educational quest epitomizes the transformative power of perseverance, dedication, and an unwavering commitment to the pursuit of excellence. His journey through various coaching roles at different universities stands as a testament to his evolution as a strategist, leader, and luminary within the realm of American football.

From the outset of his coaching career at Virginia Military Institute, Tomlin displayed an innate understanding of the game's nuances—an acumen that set him apart as a rising coaching prodigy. His role as a graduate assistant marked the genesis of a journey marked by tireless dedication and an insatiable hunger for knowledge.

Mike Tomlin

With each subsequent role at different universities, Tomlin's journey unfolded—a tapestry woven with experiences that enriched his coaching repertoire. As he traversed the landscapes of various coaching positions, from defensive back coach to wide receiver coach, the intricacies of the game became ingrained in his very being, shaping his coaching philosophy and fostering a deep appreciation for strategic thinking.

His tenure at these institutions wasn't just about wins and losses; it was a period of growth—a time where mentorship, perseverance, and the invaluable lessons learned from both victories and setbacks sculpted Tomlin into a multifaceted coach poised to leave an indelible mark on the sport.

Amidst the whirlwind of collegiate coaching roles, Tomlin's dedication to learning, adapting, and evolving was unwavering. Each experience, each season, and each team became a chapter in his coaching manual—a compendium of strategies, leadership techniques, and the invaluable art of navigating the intricate landscape of American football.

Mike Tomlin

Tomlin's collegiate odyssey wasn't merely a progression through different coaching positions; it was an expedition—and expedition where the foundations of his coaching prowess were laid, where the canvas upon which his future successes would be painted began to take shape. The mentorship he received, the challenges he faced, and the triumphs he celebrated during this journey became the cornerstones of his coaching philosophy—an amalgamation of tactics, leadership, and an unwavering commitment to the craft.

His collegiate odyssey wasn't just a stepping stone towards the pinnacle of coaching in the NFL; it was a crucible—a transformative period that imbued Tomlin with the wisdom, resilience, and strategic acumen that would define his future as a head coach and a luminary within the world of American football.

Mike Tomlin

2.1 Transition to Coaching at Virginia Military Institute

Mike Tomlin's transition to coaching at Virginia Military Institute (VMI) marked the commencement of a journey that would ultimately propel him toward the zenith of American football coaching. Within the hallowed confines of this esteemed institution, Tomlin's foray into the coaching realm began—a pivotal moment that would shape not only his career but also lay the groundwork for his future as a leader, strategist, and luminary within the sport.

As a graduate assistant at VMI, Tomlin found himself immersed in an environment steeped in tradition, discipline, and the pursuit of excellence—values that resonated deeply with his own ethos. It was here, amidst the disciplined cadence of military life and the fervor of collegiate football, that Tomlin's coaching odyssey was set in motion.

Mike Tomlin

His role as a graduate assistant wasn't merely a position; it was an opportunity—a chance to absorb the intricacies of coaching, learn from seasoned mentors, and immerse himself in the rigors of guiding young athletes toward gridiron success. Tomlin approached this role with the same dedication and passion that he had displayed as a player—a hunger for knowledge, an eagerness to contribute, and an unwavering commitment to his craft.

At VMI, Tomlin's transition to coaching became a transformative period—a time where his footballing acumen met the rigors of coaching strategy, and where the values instilled in him during his formative years found resonance in his leadership style. The experience served as a crucible—a testing ground that honed not just his coaching skills but also his ability to mentor, strategize, and inspire a team toward collective success.

His coaching philosophy at the highest levels of American football would later be defined by the discipline, resiliency, and unwavering pursuit of excellence that he learned at VMI. These lessons went beyond the confines of wins and losses.

Tomlin's tenure at Virginia Military Institute wasn't just a phase in his coaching career; it was a foundational period—a pivotal juncture where the seeds of leadership, strategy, and footballing prowess were sown. The values imbibed during his time at VMI served as the bedrock upon which his future successes would be built—an invaluable chapter in the narrative of a coach whose transition at VMI marked the genesis of an illustrious career in the world of American football coaching.

2.2 Coaching Roles at Various Universities

Mike Tomlin's coaching roles at various universities across the landscape of collegiate football served as a tapestry of experiences that shaped his trajectory toward becoming one of the NFL's premier head coaches. His journey through different coaching positions was not just

Mike Tomlin

a progression through roles but an evolution—an expedition marked by growth, resilience, and an unwavering commitment to mastering the intricacies of the game.

From his tenure as a wide receiver coach at Arkansas State University to his roles at the University of Cincinnati and the University of Memphis, Tomlin's coaching odyssey was characterized by dedication, adaptability, and an insatiable thirst for knowledge. Each coaching position became a chapter in his coaching manual—a repository of experiences that enriched his understanding of the game and honed his leadership skills.

As a young coach navigating the landscapes of collegiate football, Tomlin's roles weren't merely about devising game strategies and executing plays. They were about mentorship, player development, and the cultivation of a coaching philosophy that transcended the confines of wins and losses.

Mike Tomlin

His time at various universities afforded him the opportunity to learn from seasoned coaches, collaborate with diverse coaching staff, and navigate the intricacies of guiding young athletes through the rigors of collegiate football. Tomlin's tenure in these coaching roles became a masterclass—a period of apprenticeship where he absorbed invaluable lessons in leadership, strategy, and the art of navigating the dynamic world of American football.

Beyond the X's and O's, Tomlin's roles at these universities were a reflection of his unwavering commitment to player development, team cohesion, and the relentless pursuit of excellence. His coaching ethos became a mosaic—a combination of tactical acumen, leadership traits, and a dedication to instilling values that transcended the football field.

Each coaching role at different universities left an indelible mark on Tomlin's journey—a journey that propelled him toward the pinnacle of coaching in the NFL. The experiences garnered, the challenges faced, and the triumphs celebrated during his tenure at various universities coalesced to craft a coach poised to leave an enduring legacy within the realm of American football.

2.3 Evolving Leadership Traits and Tactical Acumen

Mike Tomlin's journey through the realms of football coaching was a testament to the evolution of his leadership traits and tactical acumen—a journey characterized by adaptability, resilience, and an unwavering dedication to mastering the intricate facets of the game.

His evolution as a leader was a narrative woven through the tapestry of his coaching roles, marked by a steadfast commitment to continuous growth and the cultivation of a coaching philosophy rooted in leadership, strategy, and unwavering determination.

Mike Tomlin

Tomlin's leadership qualities changed during his time as a coach, evolving in the harsh environment of collegiate football, and then becoming apparent when he took the helm of the Pittsburgh Steelers. He possessed a dynamic leadership style that incorporated insights from diverse team coaching experiences, lessons learned from mentors, and an unwavering commitment to excellence.

Tomlin's tactical acumen emerged as a symphony composed of strategic brilliance, adaptability, and an intuitive understanding of the game. His journey through coaching roles at various universities provided him with a canvas to refine his playbook, experiment with strategies, and craft a coaching style that mirrored the dynamism of the sport itself.

Adaptability became a cornerstone of Tomlin's coaching philosophy. His ability to evolve his strategies, adjust game plans on the fly, and inspire his teams to adapt to changing circumstances spoke volumes about his tactical acumen. Whether it was devising defensive schemes, optimizing offensive strategies, or making crucial in-game adjustments, Tomlin's proficiency in dissecting the nuances of the game became synonymous with his coaching legacy.

But beyond the X's and O's, Tomlin's leadership traits set him apart. His ability to inspire, instill discipline, and foster unity within his teams transcended the tactical aspects of coaching. It was a leadership style forged in the crucible of experiences—a mosaic comprising resilience, empathy, and an unwavering belief in the potential of his players.

He was a coach who was dedicated to the overall development of his players, to building a culture of unity and resilience, and to making a lasting legacy in the sport that extended beyond victories and defeats. His developing leadership qualities and tactical acumen were more than just tools for success on the field.

As Tomlin's journey unfolded, his leadership traits continued to evolve, his tactical acumen continued to sharpen, and his impact on the realm of American

Mike Tomlin

football continued to resonate—a testament to the enduring evolution of a coach whose leadership and tactical brilliance shaped a generation of athletes and transformed the landscape of the sport itself.

Mike Tomlin

CHAPTER 3: NFL BEGINNING

Mike Tomlin's entry into the NFL marked the inception of a new chapter in his storied coaching career—a chapter brimming with challenges, triumphs, and the indomitable spirit that would define his tenure as one of the league's most revered head coaches.

His NFL beginnings saw him take on the role of a defensive backs coach, a position that served as the gateway to the pinnacle of American football coaching. Tomlin's introduction to the NFL coaching ranks was a testament to his perseverance, strategic brilliance, and unwavering dedication to mastering the intricacies of the professional game.

After becoming the defensive backs coach for the Tampa Bay Buccaneers in 2001, Tomlin made an instant impression. He broke into the coaching scene as an up-and-coming genius known for his tactical sense and leadership abilities. His skill in working with defensive units and his natural grasp of player development helped him to achieve this.

His tenure with the Buccaneers provided Tomlin with invaluable exposure to the dynamics of coaching at the highest level. It was a period marked by mentorship under seasoned coaches, collaboration with top-tier athletes, and a deep dive into the strategies that defined success in the NFL.

Tomlin's NFL beginnings weren't merely about adapting to the rigors of professional football coaching; they were about embracing the challenges with a tenacity that mirrored his coaching philosophy. His approach wasn't just about devising game plans; it was about inspiring athletes, instilling discipline, and fostering a culture of excellence that transcended the boundaries of the football field.

Mike Tomlin

In 2006, the Pittsburgh Steelers recognized Tomlin's coaching prowess and leadership potential, appointing him as their head coach—a watershed moment that catapulted him into the echelons of NFL coaching greatness. At just 34 years old, Tomlin became the youngest head coach in Steelers' history—a testament to his capabilities, his vision, and his unyielding commitment to excellence.

His NFL beginnings as the head coach of the Pittsburgh Steelers marked the genesis of an era characterized by resilience, unity, and an unwavering pursuit of championships. Under Tomlin's stewardship, the Steelers epitomized a culture of winning, camaraderie, and the relentless pursuit of greatness—an ethos forged in the crucible of his NFL beginnings.

For Tomlin, moving up from assistant coach to head coach in the NFL was more than just a professional advancement; it was a calling. As a head coach, he had an obligation to guide, motivate, and leave a lasting impression on the professional football community. The foundation for an extraordinary coaching career that would make him a legendary coach in the NFL and leave a lasting impact on both the game and the lives he touched along the way was laid by his NFL beginnings.

3.1 Early Career in the NFL Coaching Ranks

A path characterized by commitment, strategic acumen, and an unwavering pursuit of perfection was exemplified by Mike Tomlin's early NFL coaching career. Tomlin's career path within the NFL coaching community has been a testament to his unwavering work ethic and natural coaching ability. He began his career as a defensive backs coach and rose to become one of the league's most respected head coaches.

Joining the Tampa Bay Buccaneers in 2001 as the defensive backs coach heralded Tomlin's entry into the NFL coaching landscape. It was here that he carved his niche—a young coach with an insatiable hunger for

Mike Tomlin

knowledge and a keen eye for talent development. His impact on the Buccaneers' defensive units was palpable, earning him recognition for his ability to maximize the potential of his players and contribute significantly to the team's success.

Tomlin's tenure with the Buccaneers provided the crucible for his coaching acumen to flourish. Under the mentorship of a seasoned coaching staff and in collaboration with top-tier athletes, he honed his craft, refining defensive strategies, and imbibing the intricacies of NFL coaching at its finest.

His innate ability to connect with players, inspire discipline, and foster a culture of relentless pursuit set the stage for his meteoric rise within the coaching ranks. Tomlin's approach transcended the tactical aspects of the game; it was about cultivating a winning mentality, instilling values, and fostering camaraderie—a blueprint that would later define his coaching philosophy.

Mike Tomlin

The Steelers were a model team under Tomlin, with a never-ending thirst for titles and a strong sense of camaraderie. The smooth transition from a new head coach to a leader who embodied excellence during his early years in Pittsburgh was evident. His ability to coach shaped a team and inspired a fanbase.

During Tomlin's initial years as an NFL coach, it was not just about winning and losing; it was also about developing into a leader, leaving a legacy, and leaving an impact on the game. His influence was felt throughout the history of the NFL, which is a monument to his unwavering commitment and unrelenting pursuit of greatness during his formative years.

3.2 Lessons Learned and Skills Honed

Mike Tomlin's coaching journey through the ranks of football imparted invaluable lessons and honed skills that became the bedrock of his success in the NFL. From

Mike Tomlin

his formative years as a graduate assistant to his ascension to the helm of the Pittsburgh Steelers, each step in his coaching odyssey was a masterclass in resilience, adaptability, and the relentless pursuit of excellence.

One of the foremost lessons Tomlin imbibed was the importance of adaptability. His coaching roles at various universities and his tenure with different NFL teams underscored the need to evolve, adjust strategies, and stay ahead in a dynamic and competitive landscape. This adaptability became a cornerstone of his coaching philosophy—a skill honed through experience, challenges faced, and victories celebrated.

Another crucial lesson Tomlin learned was the significance of mentorship and collaboration. His interactions with seasoned coaches, his collaborations with diverse coaching staff, and his ability to learn from those around him were pivotal in shaping his coaching ethos. Tomlin understood the power of collective wisdom, leveraging mentorship to refine his skills and

Mike Tomlin

absorb invaluable insights from the seasoned minds in the football fraternity.

Tomlin's coaching journey also sharpened his strategic acumen. His roles as a defensive backs coach, wide receiver coach, and other positions within the coaching realm were not just about devising game plans; they were about dissecting the nuances of the game, crafting intricate strategies, and optimizing player performance. His ability to analyze the game, make critical in-game adjustments, and strategize under pressure became hallmarks of his coaching style.

A crucial skill honed by Tomlin was his aptitude for player development and leadership. His approach extended beyond the tactical aspects of the sport; it encompassed inspiring and nurturing young athletes, instilling discipline, and fostering a culture of unity within teams. Tomlin's leadership skills transcended the X's and O's, emphasizing mentorship, empathy, and the empowerment of his players.

Furthermore, Tomlin learned the value of resilience and perseverance in the face of adversity. The challenges encountered in coaching—whether it was adapting to new teams, navigating tough seasons, or making critical decisions under pressure—forged a resilience that defined his coaching tenure. It was through adversity that Tomlin grew stronger, displaying unwavering determination and a steadfast commitment to success.

The amalgamation of these lessons learned and skills honed throughout his coaching journey became the pillars of Tomlin's coaching philosophy. They formed the tapestry of a coach revered for his adaptability, strategic brilliance, leadership, and unwavering dedication to excellence—a testament to the wealth of experience and the lessons ingrained in the fabric of his coaching career.

3.3 Pathway to Becoming a Defensive Strategist

Mike Tomlin

Mike Tomlin's pathway to becoming a defensive strategist was a journey etched with dedication, meticulous learning, and a profound understanding of the nuances that define defensive prowess in American football. From his early days as a graduate assistant to his pivotal roles within the NFL coaching staff, Tomlin's trajectory toward defensive mastery was a testament to his unwavering commitment to the art of defense.

The groundwork for his defensive strategy journey was established by his early actions as a graduate assistant. Tomlin studied the playbook with a fervor that would later become characteristic of his coaching style, soaking up the nuances of defensive schemes during this time. In addition to his practical experience, his thirst for knowledge allowed him to understand the tactical subtleties that make up a strong defense.

Tomlin's ascent through the coaching ranks at various universities and subsequent entry into the NFL coaching fraternity further shaped his understanding of defensive strategies. His roles as a defensive backs coach and other

Mike Tomlin

defensive-oriented positions provided him with an up-close view of the strategies, techniques, and player roles essential to crafting a robust defense.

His tenure with different teams allowed him to collaborate with defensive specialists, dissect game tapes, and fine-tune defensive game plans. Tomlin's ability to synthesize diverse defensive philosophies, adapt strategies to suit his team's strengths, and exploit opponents' weaknesses showcased his acumen as a defensive strategist.

Tomlin's extensive understanding of defensive tactics became evident when he took over as head coach of the Pittsburgh Steelers. It took a strategic mind capable of coming up with complex defensive schemes to lead one of the most respected teams in the league. Under his leadership, the Steelers' defense became a formidable force, demonstrating Tomlin's strategic acumen and defensive tactic mastery.

Mike Tomlin

Tomlin's pathway to becoming a defensive strategist wasn't just about studying playbooks or crafting game plans; it was about deciphering the psychology of the game, understanding opponents' tendencies, and leveraging his team's strengths to create an impenetrable defense. His journey epitomized the evolution of a coach whose dedication, expertise, and strategic prowess transformed defensive strategies within the realm of American football.

Mike Tomlin

CHAPTER 4: THE PITTSBURGH STEELERS ERA BEGINS

Mike Tomlin's ascension to the helm of the Pittsburgh Steelers heralded the beginning of a new era—a chapter defined by resilience, excellence, and an unwavering commitment to upholding the storied legacy of one of the NFL's most iconic franchises. His inauguration as the Steelers' head coach in 2007 marked a watershed moment in the team's history and set the stage for a transformative tenure that would etch his name among coaching luminaries.

It was an intimidating task to take over a team with a rich history and a championship history, but Tomlin approached this new chapter with his usual tenacity and vision. He started a journey that would reshape the

Mike Tomlin

team's identity and have an impact on the league at the age of 34, making him the youngest head coach in Steelers history.

Tomlin's arrival honored the core of Steelers football while also marking a break from the past. The cornerstones of his stewardship were his strategic acumen, leadership style, and unwavering commitment to the team's core values. Instilling a culture of unity, discipline, and unwavering pursuit of championships—the cornerstone of Steelers football—Tomlin embraced the legacy of the greats who came before him.

Under Tomlin's guidance, the Steelers underwent a metamorphosis, evolving into a team that embodied resilience and adaptability. His coaching philosophy transcended the X's and O's, emphasizing player development, mentorship, and a culture of accountability. The team's success wasn't merely measured in victories; it was defined by the cohesive

Mike Tomlin

spirit and unwavering resolve that Tomlin instilled within the Steelers' locker room.

His inaugural season as head coach culminated in a trip to Super Bowl XLIII—a testament to the impact he made in a short span. Though falling short of claiming the championship, Tomlin's leadership during that season underscored the resilience and mettle that would come to define his tenure.

Tomlin's Steelers were a consistent contender during his tenure, winning division titles, qualifying for the playoffs, and exemplifying grit and determination. His ability to strategically design offensive and defensive schemes as well as cultivate an excellence-oriented culture elevated the Steelers to the top of the league.

The Pittsburgh Steelers' era under Tomlin wasn't just about wins and losses; it was about resilience in the face of adversity, unity amidst challenges, and the unwavering pursuit of championships. Tomlin's impact transcended the confines of the football field, leaving an

Mike Tomlin

indelible mark on the franchise's legacy and shaping a new chapter in Steelers' history—one defined by the unwavering leadership and enduring spirit of Mike Tomlin.

4.1 Appointment as Head Coach of the Pittsburgh Steelers

Mike Tomlin's appointment as the head coach of the Pittsburgh Steelers in 2007 marked a pivotal juncture not only in his coaching career but also in the illustrious history of one of the NFL's most iconic franchises. The announcement of Tomlin's leadership ushered in an era characterized by determination, strategic brilliance, and a relentless pursuit of greatness—a new chapter that would elevate the Steelers to unprecedented heights.

At the age of 34, Tomlin became the youngest head coach in Steelers history—a testament to his prodigious talent, unwavering dedication, and the promise of a

Mike Tomlin

visionary leader poised to carve his legacy within the league. His appointment was met with both anticipation and scrutiny, tasked with shouldering the weight of upholding the Steelers' storied tradition while charting a course toward new horizons.

Stepping into the shoes of coaching legends who had graced the Steelers' sidelines before him, Tomlin embraced the challenge with a sense of purpose. His leadership style mirrored the resilience and toughness synonymous with the Steelers' ethos while infusing a modern touch, laying the foundation for an era defined by adaptability, innovation, and unwavering resolve.

Tomlin's arrival in Pittsburgh signaled more than a mere changing of the guard; it was a transformational moment—a union between a team seeking a new identity and a coach determined to leave an indelible mark on the franchise. His inauguration brought with it a breath of fresh air, igniting a renewed sense of purpose and igniting the collective spirit of the Steelers' faithful.

Mike Tomlin

Under Tomlin's tutelage, the Steelers underwent a metamorphosis, evolving into a team that mirrored the characteristics of its coach—disciplined, determined, and relentless in pursuit of victory. His coaching philosophy transcended the boundaries of the football field, emphasizing not just strategic brilliance but also player development, mentorship, and fostering a culture of unity among the roster.

The early seasons of Tomlin's tenure witnessed immediate success—a testament to his coaching acumen, strategic brilliance, and ability to connect with his players. His leadership guided the Steelers to an AFC North title in his inaugural year, setting the stage for a journey defined by consistent excellence and a perennial presence in the postseason.

The appointment of Mike Tomlin as head coach of the Pittsburgh Steelers wasn't just the beginning of a new coaching tenure; it was the inception of an era that elevated the franchise to renewed heights of success and resilience. Tomlin's impact transcended wins and losses, embodying the spirit of Steelers football and etching his name among the pantheon of coaching legends within the annals of the NFL.

4.2 Impact on Team Dynamics and Culture

Mike Tomlin's impact on team dynamics and culture within the Pittsburgh Steelers organization was nothing short of transformative. From the moment he assumed the role of head coach in 2007, Tomlin's leadership style and vision infused the team with a renewed sense of purpose, unity, and an unwavering commitment to excellence.

At the heart of Tomlin's coaching philosophy lay a deep understanding of the importance of team dynamics. He recognized that success on the field wasn't solely about individual talent but about fostering a cohesive unit—a collective spirit that transcended individual contributions. Tomlin's emphasis on teamwork,

Mike Tomlin

communication, and a shared commitment to a common goal laid the foundation for a cohesive Steelers roster.

The Steelers' culture changed under Tomlin's direction, becoming a tapestry of perseverance, self-control, and an unwavering quest for victory. His approach to leadership demonstrated an unwavering commitment to his players, instilling a sense of accountability and creating an atmosphere where each team member felt respected and empowered.

Tomlin's impact on team dynamics wasn't confined to the football field; it permeated every facet of the organization. He cultivated a culture of excellence that extended from the coaching staff to the players, from the locker room to the front office. His ability to connect with his team, to inspire discipline, and to foster unity amidst diversity became the cornerstone of Steelers football.

One of Tomlin's greatest strengths was his innate ability to mold diverse personalities into a cohesive unit. He

Mike Tomlin

understood that each player brought a unique set of skills, experiences, and perspectives to the team. Leveraging this diversity, Tomlin orchestrated a harmonious blend that celebrated individuality while promoting collective success.

The intangible elements of team dynamics, such as the players' sense of brotherhood, teammates' unwavering support, and the Steelers' indomitable spirit, were clear indicators of Tomlin's influence on team dynamics, even beyond the tactical mastery exhibited on game days. Empathy, mentoring, and a recognition that success was a team effort were the hallmarks of his coaching style.

Tomlin's imprint on team dynamics and culture within the Steelers organization wasn't just about wins, losses, or championships; it was about fostering a sense of identity, resilience, and a lasting legacy that transcended the game. His impact resonated not only within the confines of Heinz Field but also within the hearts of Steelers' fans—a testament to his ability to unite, inspire, and cultivate a culture of excellence that defined an era of Steelers football.

4.3 Setting the Stage for Success

The Pittsburgh Steelers were fortunate to have Mike Tomlin as their head coach during his tenure because of his extraordinary talent for creating winning environments, which went far beyond formulating game plans. As early as possible, Tomlin realized that creating the conditions for success required more than just tactical skill; it required an all-encompassing strategy that included culture-building, leadership, and an unwavering dedication to quality.

Upon assuming the helm in 2007, Tomlin immediately set about shaping a new narrative for the Steelers—a narrative defined by resilience, unity, and an unyielding pursuit of championships. His leadership style served as

Mike Tomlin

the linchpin for this transformation, infusing the organization with a sense of purpose and direction.

One of Tomlin's foremost strengths lies in his ability to cultivate a winning culture—a culture steeped in the values of discipline, accountability, and teamwork. He fostered an environment where every player felt valued, where diversity was celebrated, and where the collective pursuit of success superseded individual accolades.

Tomlin's vision extended beyond the X's and O's of the game. He emphasized the importance of player development, mentorship, and fostering camaraderie—a recipe that sowed the seeds for success both on and off the field. His keen understanding of team dynamics allowed him to harness the collective potential of his roster, maximizing talent and inspiring a collective spirit that propelled the Steelers forward.

Under Tomlin's stewardship, the Steelers epitomized adaptability—a quality that proved instrumental in navigating the dynamic landscape of professional football. His strategic acumen, coupled with an ability to make critical in-game adjustments, set the stage for the team's success, ensuring they remained competitive in every contest.

Tomlin's impact on setting the stage for success wasn't confined to a single facet of the organization; it permeated through every level. His emphasis on building a robust coaching staff, fostering synergy among the front office, and empowering his players to lead on and off the field solidified the foundation upon which Steelers' triumphs were built.

Furthermore, Tomlin's unrelenting pursuit of excellence became contagious—a driving force that resonated throughout the organization. His relentless commitment to raising the standard, coupled with an unwavering belief in the team's potential, set a precedent for success that inspired every member of the Steelers' family.

More important than victories or titles is the lasting impression Mike Tomlin left on the Steelers

Mike Tomlin

organization, cementing his reputation as a master at creating the conditions for success. His tenure serves as a tribute to the skill of fostering an environment of excellence, cohesion, and unwavering resolve; this legacy continues to influence the Steelers' quest for long-term success as well as their successes.

Mike Tomlin

CHAPTER 5: COACHING PHILOSOPHY UNVEILED

Mike Tomlin's coaching philosophy was a tapestry woven with the threads of leadership, resilience, adaptability, and an unwavering commitment to excellence—a blueprint that defined his tenure as one of the NFL's most revered head coaches. Unveiling his coaching philosophy wasn't merely about devising game strategies; it was about shaping a culture, fostering unity, and instilling values that transcended the football field.

The fundamental tenet of Tomlin's coaching philosophy was that team unity, rather than just individual skill, was the key to success. He promoted an environment of responsibility, self-control, and an unwavering quest for

Mike Tomlin

excellence; under his direction, this mindset became the cornerstone of Steelers football.

Tomlin's coaching ethos emphasized player development as much as tactical prowess. He believed in the holistic growth of his players—mentoring them not only in football strategies but also in life skills, instilling qualities that extended far beyond the game. His philosophy centered on nurturing individuals into not just better athletes, but better human beings, fostering a sense of responsibility and character both on and off the field.

Tomlin's coaching philosophy was characterized by its adaptability. He recognized the need for adaptability in approach and the dynamic nature of the sport. As a key component of his coaching style, Tomlin's flexibility allowed the Steelers to stay resilient and competitive in the face of adversity, whether it was through redefining team dynamics, fine-tuning strategies, or updating game plans.

Mike Tomlin

Tomlin's leadership style was characterized by empathy, mentorship, and a profound understanding of the dynamics within his team. He forged connections with his players, earning their respect and trust, fostering an environment where open communication and mutual respect thrived—a culture that empowered players to give their best on the field.

Furthermore, Tomlin's coaching philosophy extended beyond the Steelers' roster; it permeated through the entire organization. He believed in building a cohesive coaching staff, fostering collaboration, and empowering every member to contribute to the team's success—a philosophy that extended from the locker room to the front office.

Essentially, Mike Tomlin's philosophy of coaching was an expression of his diverse approach, which combined player development, leadership, flexibility, and a dedication to creating an environment of excellence. In addition to his many victories and honors, his coaching philosophy has had a lasting influence on the NFL

Mike Tomlin

coaching landscape and has shaped not only the Steelers franchise but also the organization as a whole.

5.1 Emphasis on Unity and Discipline

Mike Tomlin's coaching tenure with the Pittsburgh Steelers was defined by an unwavering emphasis on unity and discipline—a foundational pillar that underpinned the team's success and resonated throughout the organization. His coaching philosophy placed paramount importance on fostering unity among players, staff, and the entire Steelers' family while instilling a culture of discipline that became synonymous with Steelers football.

At the core of Tomlin's coaching ethos was the belief that a unified team, bound by a common purpose, could achieve extraordinary feats. He understood the significance of forging a collective spirit—a sense of brotherhood that transcended individual differences and

Mike Tomlin

celebrated diversity. Tomlin's emphasis on unity wasn't just about camaraderie on the field; it was about creating a family-like atmosphere, where every member felt valued, supported, and accountable to each other.

Discipline was a cornerstone of Tomlin's coaching philosophy. He held his players to high standards, stressing the importance of accountability, commitment, and a relentless work ethic. Tomlin's emphasis on discipline extended far beyond the gridiron—it was a way of life within the Steelers organization. Whether it was adhering to practice routines, following team protocols, or representing the Steelers with dignity and respect, discipline was ingrained in every aspect of the team's culture.

The unity and discipline fostered by Tomlin were not authoritarian; they were built on mutual respect, trust, and a shared commitment to a common goal. He cultivated an environment where players felt empowered to take ownership of their roles, supporting each other through triumphs and setbacks—a culture that

Mike Tomlin

transcended individual egos and propelled the team toward collective success.

Tomlin's leadership style exemplified a balance between fostering unity and instilling discipline. He forged connections with his players, earning their trust and respect, while holding them to the highest standards of professionalism. His ability to navigate the delicate balance between being a mentor and a disciplinarian underscored his effectiveness as a leader.

The emphasis on unity and discipline within the Steelers' organization wasn't just a formula for on-field success; it was a philosophy that echoed through the annals of Steelers history. It became a legacy—a legacy of a coach who understood the power of unity in achieving greatness, who instilled discipline as the cornerstone of success, and whose impact extended far beyond wins and losses, shaping the very identity of Steelers football.

Mike Tomlin

5.2 Building a Winning Culture

Mike Tomlin's tenure as the head coach of the Pittsburgh Steelers was characterized by his unparalleled ability to build and sustain a winning culture—a culture that transcended mere victories on the football field. From the moment he assumed leadership in 2007, Tomlin embarked on a mission to foster an environment where success was not just an aspiration but an ingrained ethos within the organization.

Central to Tomlin's blueprint for success was the cultivation of a winning mindset—a mentality that permeated every aspect of the Steelers' operation. He instilled a belief that winning wasn't just a result of actions on game day; it was a culmination of everyday choices, habits, and a collective commitment to excellence.

At the heart of building a winning culture was Tomlin's unwavering emphasis on values. He championed

Mike Tomlin

discipline, accountability, and a tireless work ethic as non-negotiable components of Steelers football. Tomlin's emphasis on these values laid the groundwork for a culture where every player, coach, and staff member understood the standards expected of them.

Tomlin's leadership was instrumental in shaping the winning culture within the Steelers' locker room. He connected with his players on a personal level, earning their trust and respect while challenging them to elevate their game. His ability to inspire, motivate, and galvanize the team towards a common goal became a cornerstone of the Steelers' success.

Moreover, Tomlin understood that building a winning culture required fostering a sense of unity—a cohesive spirit that bound the team together. He nurtured an environment where players supported each other, celebrated successes together, and weathered challenges as a unified front. This sense of camaraderie, solidarity, and mutual respect became the bedrock upon which Steelers football thrived.

Tomlin's commitment to building a winning culture extended beyond the confines of the football field. He emphasized character development, personal growth, and the importance of contributing positively to the community—a testament to his belief that true success extended beyond the scoreboard.

The Steelers, led by Tomlin, were more than just a team focused on winning; they represented a culture that valued resiliency, cohesion, and an unwavering quest for excellence. As a creator of a winning culture, he left an enduring legacy that continues to inspire generations of football players as well as those outside of the sport. His impact was felt not only on the Steelers organization but also on the essence of what it meant to have a winning mentality.

5.3 Transformative Approach to Leadership

Mike Tomlin

Mike Tomlin's transformative approach to leadership stands as a testament to his unparalleled ability to inspire, innovate, and cultivate an environment where greatness thrives. From the outset of his tenure as the head coach of the Pittsburgh Steelers, Tomlin's leadership style was a beacon of change—a paradigm that redefined what it meant to lead a team in the world of professional football.

At the heart of Tomlin's leadership was his innate capacity to connect with people. He possessed an uncanny ability to relate to his players, coaches, and staff on a personal level—forging bonds built on trust, respect, and genuine understanding. Tomlin's approach wasn't just about commanding authority; it was about fostering relationships, creating a culture of empathy, and instilling confidence in his team.

Tomlin's leadership went beyond the traditional mold. He embraced innovation, adapting his coaching style to resonate with the evolving dynamics of the game and the changing needs of his players. He understood that

Mike Tomlin

effective leadership wasn't static—it demanded agility, flexibility, and a willingness to evolve. Tomlin's transformative approach was a testament to his openness to new ideas and his constant quest for improvement.

A hallmark of Tomlin's leadership was his unwavering belief in empowering his team. He fostered an environment where every member felt valued, heard, and entrusted with a sense of ownership. Tomlin's empowerment wasn't just about delegating tasks; it was about creating leaders within the team, nurturing a culture where everyone felt responsible for the collective success of the Steelers.

Tomlin's leadership style was characterized by a relentless pursuit of excellence. He set high standards, challenged his team to push their limits, and led by example. His work ethic, determination, and dedication served as a source of inspiration—an embodiment of the standards he set for his players and staff.

Mike Tomlin

Furthermore, Tomlin's transformative leadership extended beyond the football field. He emphasized character development, fostering a culture of integrity, and encouraging his team to be positive influences within their communities. His leadership legacy wasn't just about wins and losses; it was about instilling values that transcended the game.

In essence, Mike Tomlin's transformative approach to leadership redefined the narrative of coaching in the NFL. His ability to connect, innovate, empower, and drive his team towards greatness stands as a testament to his enduring impact. Tomlin's legacy as a transformative leader continues to inspire not just within the realm of football but as a model for leadership excellence in all areas of life.

CHAPTER 6: ACHIEVEMENTS

Mike Tomlin's coaching career stands adorned with a tapestry of milestones and achievements that etched his name among the NFL's coaching elite. From his inaugural days as the head coach of the Pittsburgh Steelers to his consistent impact over the years, Tomlin's journey has been marked by significant milestones and unparalleled accomplishments.

Tomlin made history as the youngest head coach to lead the Steelers at the beginning of his coaching career in 2007; this accomplishment highlighted his extraordinary talent and visionary leadership. Two years later, he became the youngest head coach to win a Super Bowl championship, having guided the Steelers to the Super Bowl that same season. His victory in Super Bowl XLIII marked a significant turning point in his coaching career.

Mike Tomlin

Tomlin's early success was a prelude to a string of accomplishments that defined his coaching tenure. Under his guidance, the Steelers clinched division titles, made multiple playoff appearances, and remained a perennial contender in the ultra-competitive landscape of the NFL. His consistent ability to lead the team to postseason success and maintain a high level of competitiveness attested to his coaching acumen and strategic brilliance.

Beyond the accolades, Tomlin's milestones were reflective of his enduring impact on the Steelers' franchise. He reached the impressive feat of 100 regular-season wins in the shortest time in Steelers' history, cementing his status as one of the most successful head coaches in the organization's storied history.

Moreover, Tomlin's milestones extended beyond statistical achievements. He became the first coach in Steelers' history to guide the team to six AFC North

Mike Tomlin

division titles—a testament to his sustained excellence in a highly competitive division.

Tomlin's achievements were not confined to on-field success. He earned the respect of his peers, garnering accolades and recognition as a leader in the coaching fraternity. His contributions to the game earned him admiration, not just for wins and championships, but for his transformative approach to coaching, leadership, and his commitment to excellence both on and off the field.

Mike Tomlin's accomplishments and anniversaries, taken together, essentially sum up a coaching career that goes beyond numbers and awards. Within the Steelers organization and throughout the professional football landscape, they represent a legacy of leadership, tenacity, and an unwavering pursuit of greatness.

6.1 Division Titles and Playoff Appearances

Mike Tomlin

Mike Tomlin's coaching tenure with the Pittsburgh Steelers was a testament to his consistent success in clinching division titles and making impactful playoff appearances—a testament to his leadership, strategic brilliance, and unwavering commitment to excellence. Throughout his years at the helm, Tomlin's Steelers consistently found themselves among the NFL's elite, marked by their dominance within the AFC North and their perennial presence in the postseason.

Under Tomlin's guidance, the Steelers became a force to be reckoned with in the ultra-competitive AFC North division. His ability to lead the team to victory in one of the NFL's toughest divisions was a testament to his strategic prowess and his team's resilience. Tomlin steered the Steelers to a remarkable six AFC North division titles—a feat that solidified the team's supremacy within their division and underscored their consistency in achieving success year after year.

Beyond their divisional triumphs, Tomlin's Steelers were a constant presence in the NFL playoffs. His adeptness at

Mike Tomlin

navigating the grueling regular season, making critical in-game adjustments, and preparing his team for postseason contention showcased his coaching acumen. The Steelers' frequent appearances in the playoffs under Tomlin's leadership mirrored the team's commitment to sustained excellence and their ability to thrive in high-stakes scenarios.

Tomlin's Steelers were perennial contenders in the quest for the Lombardi Trophy. His leadership guided the team to multiple playoff appearances, positioning them as formidable challengers on the road to the Super Bowl. Their presence in the postseason became synonymous with a brand of football characterized by resilience, adaptability, and a relentless pursuit of championship glory.

Each playoff appearance and division title under Tomlin's stewardship was a testament to the culture he fostered within the Steelers' organization—a culture built on unity, discipline, and an unwavering pursuit of greatness. His ability to consistently lead the team to the

Mike Tomlin

playoffs and clinch division titles spoke volumes about his coaching acumen, his ability to maximize the potential of his roster, and his knack for guiding the Steelers to success in the face of formidable competition.

In essence, Mike Tomlin's legacy of division titles and playoff appearances wasn't just a tally of statistics; it was a reflection of his enduring impact on the Steelers' franchise. His consistent ability to lead the team to postseason contention and clinch divisional crowns exemplified his legacy as a coach who set the standard for sustained excellence and championship-caliber football within the AFC North and the NFL as a whole.

6.2 Super Bowl Victory in Super Bowl XLIII

Mike Tomlin's crowning achievement as the head coach of the Pittsburgh Steelers came in the exhilarating victory at Super Bowl XLIII—an iconic moment that etched his name in NFL history and solidified his legacy

Mike Tomlin

as a masterful leader and strategist. The road to Super Bowl XLIII was paved with challenges, but Tomlin's unwavering guidance and strategic brilliance propelled the Steelers to a triumphant victory on football's grandest stage.

Super Bowl XLIII was a spectacle that showcased the epitome of Tomlin's coaching prowess. Facing the Arizona Cardinals, the Steelers were poised for a clash that would define legacies and create indelible memories. Tomlin's leadership became the linchpin that unified his team, forging a collective determination to seize the championship.

The game itself was a testament to the Steelers' resilience and Tomlin's strategic acumen. It was a high-stakes battle that saw both teams trading blows in a contest that exemplified the essence of championship football. Tomlin's ability to make crucial in-game adjustments, maintain composure under pressure, and guide his team through adversity proved pivotal in securing victory.

Mike Tomlin

The defining moment of Super Bowl XLIII came in the game's waning moments—an iconic play etched in NFL lore. With the Steelers trailing, quarterback Ben Roethlisberger orchestrated a drive for the ages, culminating in Santonio Holmes' acrobatic, toe-tapping catch in the corner of the end zone. It was a moment that encapsulated the Steelers' resilience, Tomlin's unwavering faith in his team, and the sheer determination to claim victory.

The triumph in Super Bowl XLIII wasn't just about the Lombardi Trophy; it was a testament to Tomlin's leadership style—a fusion of mentorship, resilience, and an unyielding pursuit of excellence. His ability to inspire his team, navigate the complexities of a championship game, and orchestrate victory against a formidable opponent underscored his mastery as a coach.

Beyond the glitz of the championship, the victory in Super Bowl XLIII was a culmination of Tomlin's relentless pursuit of greatness. It was a testament to his ability to cultivate a winning culture, foster unity among his players, and guide the Steelers to the pinnacle of NFL success.

Super Bowl XLIII remains a cherished chapter in NFL history—a chapter that immortalized Mike Tomlin's legacy as a Super Bowl-winning head coach, etching his name among the coaching greats and solidifying his place in football lore as a leader who steered his team to championship glory on football's grandest stage.

6.3 Tomlin's Mark on Steelers' History

The impact that Mike Tomlin has had on the Pittsburgh Steelers goes beyond numbers and awards; his legacy is ingrained in the team's culture and endures throughout the team's history. Tomlin began a journey that would mold the character of one of the NFL's most legendary teams as soon as he took over as head coach, leaving a lasting impression that reverberates throughout Heinz Field and beyond.

Mike Tomlin

Tomlin's tenure was defined by a resounding commitment to excellence—an unwavering pursuit of greatness that became synonymous with Steelers football under his stewardship. He ushered in a new era of success, building upon the foundation laid by coaching legends before him while infusing a modern touch, adaptability, and a visionary leadership style that set the Steelers on a path to sustained prominence.

His leadership wasn't just about victories and championships; it was about fostering a culture—a culture characterized by unity, discipline, and a relentless pursuit of championship glory. Tomlin's Steelers became emblematic of resilience—a team that thrived amidst adversity, a team that embraced challenges as opportunities, and a team that embodied the steel city's indomitable spirit.

Tomlin's mark on Steelers' history extended beyond on-field success; it was about nurturing a brotherhood—a sense of camaraderie that bound players, coaches, and fans together. He fostered an environment

Mike Tomlin

where the Steelers' faithful saw their values mirrored on the gridiron—toughness, resilience, and an unyielding commitment to each other.

The Steelers were one of the NFL's most consistent teams under Tomlin's leadership, winning division titles, going to multiple postseasons, and finishing as regular contenders. He demonstrated leadership, flexibility, and a talent for navigating the Steelers through the shifting tides of professional football by leading the team through victories and defeats.

Moreover, Tomlin's impact transcended the confines of the football field. He became a symbol of hope, inspiration, and leadership excellence—a coach whose influence extended far beyond wins and losses, leaving an enduring legacy that resonates with Steelers fans worldwide.

Mike Tomlin's impact on the history of the Steelers is essentially a saga—a tale of leadership, tenacity, and an unwavering dedication to excellence. His legacy—which

Mike Tomlin

will always be treasured in the annals of Pittsburgh Steelers football history—continues to shape the identity of the team, capturing the spirit of what it means to bleed black and gold.

Mike Tomlin

CHAPTER 7: LEADERSHIP BEYOND THE GAME

Mike Tomlin's leadership extends far beyond the realms of football, transcending the confines of the game to impact communities, inspire individuals, and exemplify the essence of true leadership in its most profound sense. Beyond the X's and O's, his influence reverberates through society, leaving an indelible mark that extends well beyond the gridiron.

Tomlin's leadership prowess isn't confined to the football field; it's a beacon of inspiration that radiates in the broader scope of life. His commitment to excellence, resilience, and unity sets a precedent for aspiring leaders across various spheres. His legacy isn't solely about wins

Mike Tomlin

and championships; it's about the character he embodies and the values he espouses.

One of the hallmarks of Tomlin's leadership beyond the game lies in his emphasis on character development and community impact. He has been a guiding force in empowering athletes to be positive role models, contributing to society, and using their platform for social change. Through various philanthropic endeavors and community engagement initiatives, Tomlin's leadership instills the importance of giving back and inspiring others to make a difference.

Moreover, Tomlin's leadership transcends boundaries, resonating with individuals from diverse backgrounds. His ability to connect with people, inspire greatness, and promote unity serves as a beacon of hope, transcending differences and fostering a sense of inclusivity and belonging.

Tomlin's leadership style embodies empathy, mentorship, and a deep commitment to nurturing the potential of

Mike Tomlin

individuals beyond the realm of sports. His guidance extends to mentoring young leaders, imparting invaluable lessons in resilience, teamwork, and dedication that extend far beyond the football field.

Furthermore, Tomlin's leadership legacy extends to future generations, inspiring young athletes to not only excel in sports but also embody the principles of integrity, discipline, and perseverance. His influence as a role model shapes the values of tomorrow's leaders, nurturing a generation that values teamwork, resilience, and a relentless pursuit of their aspirations.

Mike Tomlin is a mentor, a philanthropist, and an advocate for positive change, and his leadership beyond the game embodies all of the qualities of a transformative leader. His impact on society goes beyond victories and defeats; it is a monument to the lasting influence of leadership that uplifts, empowers, and leaves a lasting impression. Tomlin's leadership transcends sports; it's a source of inspiration that shows the way to greatness, harmony, and constructive change for everybody.

7.1 Mentorship and Player Development

Mike Tomlin's legacy as a coach extends far beyond wins and losses; it's defined by his profound mentorship and commitment to player development—a testament to his belief in nurturing not just athletes but individuals, fostering growth, and instilling lifelong values that transcend the game of football.

Tomlin's coaching focused on developing players' character and realizing their potential off the field in addition to helping them on the field. To many players who wore the black and gold of the Pittsburgh Steelers, he was a mentor, a leader, and an inspiration.

Tomlin gave the players more than just a coach; he was a mentor who cared about their development, had faith in their skills, and pushed them to be the best they could be off the field. His guidance was marked by compassion, comprehension, and an unwavering dedication to the player's overall development.

Tomlin's approach to player development was multifaceted. He recognized that developing players went beyond refining their football skills; it involved cultivating life skills, instilling discipline, and fostering a sense of responsibility. His emphasis on character development, integrity, and resilience became the cornerstone of his player development philosophy.

Moreover, Tomlin's mentorship extended beyond football strategy—it was about preparing individuals for life beyond the game. He emphasized the importance of education, personal growth, and contributing positively to society, nurturing well-rounded individuals poised for success beyond their playing careers.

Tomlin's impact on player development and mentorship extended to shaping the careers of emerging talents. His

Mike Tomlin

guidance helped mold rookies into seasoned professionals, transforming raw potential into polished skills. His mentorship created an environment where players thrived, pushed their limits, and evolved into leaders in their own right.

His mentorship legacy isn't just about the success stories on the field; it's about the lasting impact he made on individuals' lives. The lessons learned under Tomlin's guidance—resilience in the face of adversity, the value of teamwork, and the importance of character—echo through the lives of those he mentored.

A legacy of investing in people, fostering their potential, and instilling values that go beyond the game of football is essentially represented by Mike Tomlin's player development and mentoring. The players who were fortunate enough to receive his guidance have seen his influence far beyond the field, leaving a legacy that epitomizes leadership, mentoring, and the enormous benefits of investing in the development of others.

Mike Tomlin

7.2 Advocacy for Social Causes

Mike Tomlin's influence is evident in his advocacy for social causes and his willingness to use his platform to effect positive change in areas of society beyond sports. His influence is felt far beyond the football field.

Tomlin became well-known as a social activist during his time as the head coach of the Pittsburgh Steelers, using his position to support a number of programs meant to promote development. His advocacy emphasized that a leader's responsibilities go beyond the football field and include addressing social injustices, advancing education, and strengthening communities.

Tomlin's advocacy was characterized by a genuine commitment to making a difference. He understood the power of his platform and used it to raise awareness and support for causes close to his heart. Whether addressing issues of racial inequality, promoting education and youth development, or supporting initiatives that uplifted

Mike Tomlin

underserved communities, Tomlin's voice resonated as a beacon of hope and inspiration.

His advocacy for social causes wasn't just a public statement; it was ingrained in his actions and involvement within communities. Tomlin actively engaged in philanthropic endeavors, supporting organizations and initiatives that sought to address social challenges, empower individuals, and create opportunities for positive change.

Moreover, Tomlin's leadership extended to fostering conversations about pressing societal issues within the realm of sports. He encouraged dialogue, promoted understanding, and emphasized the importance of unity and empathy in addressing social challenges—a stance that echoed his commitment to using sports as a catalyst for positive change in society.

Tomlin's advocacy for social causes wasn't confined to a single initiative or moment; it was a consistent thread woven into the fabric of his leadership. He inspired others within the NFL and beyond to use their influence for good, exemplifying the essence of a leader who recognizes the platform bestowed upon him and utilizes it as a force for positive transformation.

Mike Tomlin's advocacy for social causes stands as a testament to his leadership beyond the game. His commitment to making a difference, raising awareness, and supporting causes aimed at societal betterment embodies the true essence of using one's influence to effect positive change—a legacy that transcends football and resonates as an inspiration for leaders in all spheres of life.

7.3 Inspirational Impact Beyond Football

Mike Tomlin's inspirational impact extends far beyond the boundaries of football, transcending the realm of sports to become a beacon of inspiration for individuals from all walks of life. His leadership, resilience, and

Mike Tomlin

unwavering commitment to excellence resonate as a source of motivation, guiding principles, and an embodiment of what it means to strive for greatness in any endeavor.

Tomlin's impact transcends the confines of the gridiron, influencing individuals across diverse spheres. His journey—from a groundbreaking head coach to a revered figure in sports—serves as a testament to the power of dedication, hard work, and perseverance in achieving one's aspirations.

His leadership style, characterized by empathy, mentorship, and an unyielding pursuit of excellence, inspires individuals to lead by example, fostering unity, and nurturing the potential of those around them. Tomlin's leadership philosophy serves as a blueprint for aspiring leaders, emphasizing the importance of character, resilience, and the ability to inspire and uplift others.

Mike Tomlin

Tomlin's resilience in the face of challenges embodies the spirit of overcoming obstacles, inspiring individuals to confront adversity with courage and determination. His ability to navigate through setbacks and emerge stronger speaks volumes about the importance of resilience in the pursuit of success.

Tomlin's impact extends to mentoring and empowering young talents, instilling in them the values of discipline, teamwork, and dedication. His mentorship goes beyond football strategy, nurturing individuals into becoming well-rounded, responsible, and principled leaders in their own right.

Beyond his coaching achievements, Tomlin's advocacy for social causes and community engagement sets an example for individuals to use their influence to drive positive change. His commitment to addressing societal issues and making a difference highlights the responsibility of leaders to contribute to the betterment of society.

Mike Tomlin

Mike Tomlin's inspirational impact transcends the boundaries of football, resonating as a symbol of leadership, resilience, and the relentless pursuit of excellence. His legacy inspires individuals to strive for greatness, fostering a spirit of unity, empowerment, and positive transformation—a legacy that continues to motivate and uplift countless individuals, both within and outside the realm of sports.

Mike Tomlin

CHAPTER 8: ENDURING LEGACY

Mike Tomlin left an enduring legacy that goes beyond football, leaving an enduring impression on the game, the Pittsburgh Steelers franchise, and the leadership community at large. This legacy is an intricate tapestry woven with the threads of leadership, resilience, mentorship, and an unwavering commitment to excellence.

At the core of Tomlin's legacy lies his exemplary leadership—a beacon of inspiration that illuminated paths toward greatness. His tenure as the head coach of the Steelers was defined not just by wins and championships, but by the culture he fostered—a culture grounded in unity, discipline, and an unrelenting pursuit of success.

Mike Tomlin

Tomlin's legacy is a testament to his resilience—the ability to weather storms, overcome challenges, and emerge stronger. His leadership shone brightest during moments of adversity, where he steered the Steelers through turbulent times with unwavering determination, inspiring his team to rise above challenges and strive for excellence.

His enduring legacy extends beyond the confines of football strategy; it encompasses mentorship—an investment in individuals that transcends the game. Tomlin's mentorship nurtured not only football talent but also character, fostering leaders on and off the field, and leaving an indelible imprint on the lives of those he guided.

Furthermore, Tomlin's enduring legacy encompasses his advocacy for social causes, emphasizing the responsibility of leaders to use their platform for positive change. His commitment to addressing societal issues and empowering communities speaks volumes about the impact of leadership beyond the game of football.

Mike Tomlin

A mentor, a visionary, and a role model whose influence goes far beyond wins and losses, Tomlin's legacy goes far beyond numbers and accolades. The ideals of honesty, fortitude, and the unrelenting pursuit of greatness are emphasized in his legacy, which serves as a beacon of guidance for future leaders.

A legacy of leadership excellence, Mike Tomlin transcends time and leaves an enduring imprint on the history of football and leadership globally. His legacy isn't limited to any one moment or accomplishment; rather, it is an inspiration, a guide, and a force to be reckoned with in the future of leadership in sports, communities, and beyond.

8.1 Tomlin's Influence

Mike Tomlin's influence and impact are woven into the very fabric of the NFL, shaping the landscape of football

Mike Tomlin

and leadership in profound ways that extend far beyond the sidelines. From his groundbreaking achievements to his unwavering commitment to excellence, Tomlin's influence resonates as a defining force that has left an indelible mark on the sport and beyond.

As the head coach of the Pittsburgh Steelers, Tomlin's impact reverberates through the annals of football history. His leadership style, characterized by a unique blend of mentorship, resilience, and unwavering dedication, became a guiding light for aspiring coaches and leaders across the league. Tomlin's ability to connect with players, nurture talent, and steer his team through both triumphs and setbacks set a benchmark for leadership excellence.

His influence extends beyond wins and losses, emphasizing the importance of character development, discipline, and a relentless pursuit of excellence. Tomlin's impact on player development transcends the game itself, shaping individuals into not just stellar

Mike Tomlin

athletes but principled leaders poised for success in all facets of life.

Furthermore, Tomlin's influence is felt in the broader scope of society. His advocacy for social causes underscores the role of sports figures as catalysts for positive change. His commitment to addressing societal issues, promoting education, and empowering communities set an example for leaders across all spheres, highlighting the power of using one's platform for the greater good.

Tomlin's influence extends to mentoring emerging talents, inspiring the next generation of leaders, and fostering a culture of inclusivity and unity. His impact as a role model and mentor continues to shape the lives of countless individuals, instilling values of integrity, perseverance, and the importance of making a positive impact on society.

Mike Tomlin is a prime example of leadership excellence and the enormous impact one person can have

Mike Tomlin

on an entire industry. His influence and impact go far beyond the realm of football. His legacy acts as a beacon of hope, encouraging leaders to pursue greatness, change the world, and leave a lasting impression on future generations. This is evidence of the transformative power of leadership, both on and off the field.

8.2 Reflections on Coaching Philosophy

Mike Tomlin's coaching philosophy is a complex fabric made of a multitude of encounters, insights gained, and a strong conviction in the fundamental principles that characterize his style of coaching. It is a philosophy that reflects the principles of resilience, leadership, and an unwavering quest for excellence.

At the heart of Tomlin's coaching philosophy lies the unwavering belief in fostering a culture of unity and discipline. He emphasizes the importance of creating a cohesive environment where every individual

Mike Tomlin

understands their role, works cohesively as a team, and embodies the values that define Steelers football—resilience, toughness, and an unrelenting commitment to excellence.

Tomlin's coaching philosophy extends beyond the X's and O's of the game. He recognizes the significance of character development, instilling in his players the values of integrity, accountability, and perseverance. His coaching isn't just about winning games; it's about nurturing individuals into well-rounded leaders, preparing them for success both on and off the field.

Furthermore, Tomlin's coaching philosophy is a testament to adaptability and flexibility. He understands the ever-evolving nature of the game and emphasizes the importance of adjusting strategies to meet the dynamic challenges that arise. His ability to make in-game adjustments, adapt to changing circumstances, and motivate his team amidst adversity reflects the core principles of his coaching philosophy.

Mike Tomlin

Tomlin's coaching philosophy also centers on mentorship—a commitment to guiding and empowering individuals to reach their full potential. He fosters an environment where players feel supported, valued, and entrusted with the responsibility to lead, creating a legacy of leaders within his team.

Tomlin's coaching philosophy is grounded in the pursuit of greatness—an unrelenting pursuit of excellence that permeates every aspect of his coaching. He instills in his team a mindset that embraces challenges, refuses to settle for mediocrity, and constantly strives for improvement.

Mike Tomlin's reflections on coaching philosophy epitomize the essence of transformative leadership—a philosophy built on unity, resilience, mentorship, and an unyielding pursuit of greatness. His approach transcends the game of football, serving as a guiding light for aspiring coaches and leaders, emphasizing the values and principles that define success both on and off the field—an enduring legacy that continues to inspire and shape the landscape of coaching in sports and beyond.

8.3 Contributions to Football's Pantheon of Greats

The fact that Mike Tomlin is included in the pantheon of football greats is evidence of his lasting influence, revolutionary leadership, and deep impact, all of which have left a lasting impression on the history of the game. His rise from an innovative head coach to a highly regarded figure in the NFL is evidence of his accomplishments that reach far beyond the football field.

Tomlin's legacy is etched in the annals of football as a coach whose impact transcends statistics and trophies. His leadership style, characterized by resilience, mentorship, and an unwavering pursuit of excellence, has redefined the standards of coaching greatness.

Mike Tomlin

His contributions to football extend beyond wins and losses; they embody a legacy of unity—a unity that fostered a culture of brotherhood within the Pittsburgh Steelers and served as a blueprint for success. Tomlin's teams epitomize resilience, embodying the steel city's spirit and resilience in the face of adversity—a legacy that reverberates through the ethos of Steelers football.

Tomlin's contributions are intertwined with mentorship—a commitment to nurturing talent, shaping character, and empowering individuals to become leaders both on and off the field. His mentorship extends beyond football strategy, emphasizing the importance of values, integrity, and perseverance.

His impact extends to the broader landscape of the NFL. Tomlin's advocacy for social causes, community engagement, and leadership beyond the game underscores the responsibility of sports figures to effect positive change. His commitment to addressing societal issues and using his platform for social good sets an example for leaders across all spheres.

Mike Tomlin

Tomlin's contributions are a reflection of the transformative power of leadership—a legacy that inspires aspiring coaches, leaders, and athletes to strive for greatness, embrace challenges, and leave a lasting impact on the sport and society.

A legacy of leadership excellence, tenacity, and a profound impact that goes well beyond the game characterizes Mike Tomlin's contributions to football's pantheon of greats. This legacy inspires future generations of NFL players and serves as a beacon of guidance for the sport.

Mike Tomlin

CONCLUSION

In the final pages of Mike Tomlin: The Maestro of the Gridiron, we find ourselves reflecting on the extraordinary journey of a coaching virtuoso. As the chapters unfolded, the portrait of Mike Tomlin emerged not just as a football coach but as a maestro, orchestrating a symphony of talent, strategy, and leadership on the gridiron.

Tomlin's coaching philosophy, revealed through pivotal moments and strategic decisions, showcased an unwavering commitment to excellence. The field became his stage, and each player, a crucial note in the melody of success. The resounding echoes of victories and the humbling lessons of defeats painted a canvas of resilience and adaptability.

We learned about Tomlin's distinct leadership style throughout the story, which combined empathy and authority to establish discipline and promote teamwork.

Mike Tomlin

His capacity to establish a personal connection with players went beyond the typical coach-player dynamic and fostered a culture of fraternity and unity.

As we close the book, the echoes of Tomlin's impactful speeches and halftime talks linger in our minds. The maestro's words were not just motivational; they were a testament to his profound understanding of the human spirit and the art of motivation. The locker room became a sanctuary where belief in oneself and trust in the team converged.

Beyond the Xs and Os, we witnessed Tomlin's commitment to social justice, his advocacy for equality, and his role as a mentor extending beyond the football field. The maestro's influence reached far beyond wins and losses, resonating in the lives he touched and the values he instilled.

In the grand finale, Mike Tomlin: The Maestro of the Gridiron leaves us with a sense of admiration for a coach who transcended the boundaries of his profession.

Mike Tomlin

Tomlin's legacy is not just etched in the record books but in the hearts of players, fans, and football enthusiasts alike. The maestro's symphony continues to play, a timeless ode to leadership, resilience, and the enduring spirit of the gridiron.

Made in the USA
Monee, IL
04 December 2024